THE WORLD OF ENERGY

Understanding
SOLAR
POWER

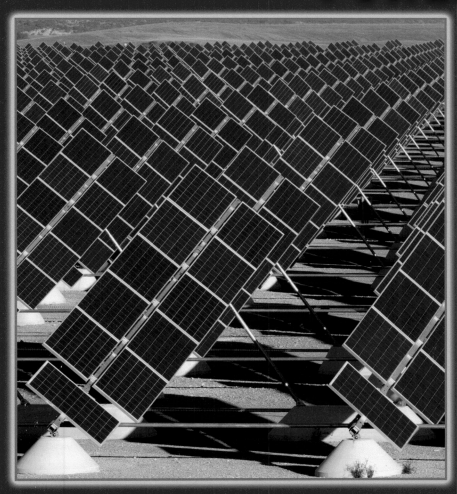

FIONA REYNOLDSON

D1363983

Gareth Stevens
Publishing

Please visit our Web site, www.garethstevens.com. For a free color catalog of all our high-quality books, call toll free 1-800-542-2595 or fax 1-877-542-2596.

Library of Congress Cataloging-in-Publication Data

Reynoldson, Fiona.
Understanding solar power / Fiona Reynoldson.
    p. cm. — (The world of energy)
Includes index.
ISBN 978-1-4339-4127-6 (library binding)
1. Solar energy—Juvenile literature. I. Title.
TJ810.3.R46 2011
621.47—dc22
                                2010015848

This edition first published in 2011 by
Gareth Stevens Publishing
111 East 14th Street, Suite 349
New York, NY 10003

Copyright © 2011 Wayland/Gareth Stevens Publishing

Editorial Director: Kerri O'Donnell
Art Director: Haley Harasymiw

Photo Credits:
Corbis 31 (Patrick Byrd), 34 (bottom) (Tim Dornin/epa), 35 (Bob Daemmrich); James Davis Travel Photography: 9, 20–21; Ecoscene 5 (Mitch Kezar) 10, 25 (Brown), 30 (Erik Schaffer); Eye Ubiquitous: 12 (Brian Harding), 18 (Mark Newham); Mary Evans Picture Library: 14; Flickr/Gnal 41 (top); Frank Lane Picture Agency: 13; Ole Steen Hansen: 28, 29 (top); James Hawkins/Oxfam UK: 38, 38–39, 39; NASA 44; Science Photo Library 22–23 (David Nunuk), 23 (David Nunuk); Shell Photo Library/Solavolt International: 29 (bottom); Shutterstock *cover* and 1 (Pedro Salaverria); Stockmarket/Zefa: 15, 26, 36, 40–41 (Joe Soh m); UKAEA/AEA Technology: pages 19, 24, 36–37; US Department of Energy: 4, 7, 32–33, 34 (top).

Printed in China
CPSIA compliance information: Batch #WAS10GS: For further information contact Gareth Stevens, New York, New York at 1-800-542-2595.

CONTENTS

What Is Solar Power?

Sunshine and Solar Power

Every 15 minutes, the Earth receives enough energy from the sun to power everything on our planet for a whole year. Yet only a tiny amount of the energy we use in our daily lives comes directly from the sun. Currently, making electricity from sunlight is expensive.

Fossil Fuels or Solar Power?

Oil, coal, and gas are called fossil fuels. They give up their stored energy easily, when they are burned. They can be used to make electricity cheaply.

Problems with Fossil Fuels

There are problems with fossil fuels:
- When they are burned, they pollute the air.
- We are using a lot of them for fuel. There may be none left soon.

Nuclear Power, Fossil Fuels, or Solar Power?

Nuclear power is cleaner than fossil fuels. However, it produces dangerous radioactive waste. We need to find cheaper ways to use solar power (the energy from sunlight). Sunlight is a clean and renewable source of energy. This book looks at ways in which it can be used.

This U.S. Navy test platform gets electricity from solar panels (below) and a wind turbine (above).▼

Life on Earth is only possible because of energy from the sun. ▼

FACT FILE

FOSSIL FUELS

How much is left?
Some scientists think
we have:

- about 40 years of oil
- about 60 years of natural gas
- about 300 years of coal.

The sun is so big that more than one million Earths would fit inside it. Because it is so big, there are huge pressures inside it. These huge pressures make very high temperatures.

The Sun—a Nuclear Reactor

The sun is like a nuclear reactor out in space. It is a nuclear reactor that works by nuclear fusion.

Violent eruptions from the sun release huge bursts of energy and particles. Even a small eruption can be as powerful as a million nuclear bombs. ▼

WHAT IS NUCLEAR FUSION?
Nuclei hit each other so fast that they stick together. This releases energy and one neutron particle. (Nuclei is the plural of nucleus.) ▼

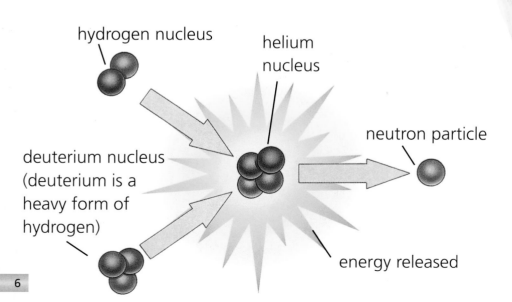

hydrogen nucleus

helium nucleus

neutron particle

deuterium nucleus (deuterium is a heavy form of hydrogen)

energy released

Nuclear Fusion in the Sun

In the sun, hydrogen atoms crash into each other. They crash so hard that they stick together. This makes a different element called helium. This type of reaction is called nuclear fusion (see the diagram on page 6). Huge amounts of energy turn into heat and light. This energy streams out into space. Some of this solar energy reaches the Earth.

Mirrors concentrate sunlight onto a transparent tube. The solar power helps to purify the contaminated water that is pumped through the tube. ▶

Electromagnetic Waves

Heat and light are made up of electrical waves and magnetic waves. These waves travel from the sun like waves across the sea. Some of them hit the Earth. The light that leaves the sun takes eight minutes to reach the Earth.

Most of the solar energy (heat and light from the sun) is soaked up by the sea and land near the Equator. This land heats up so the water evaporates. This makes hot, sandy deserts. ▼

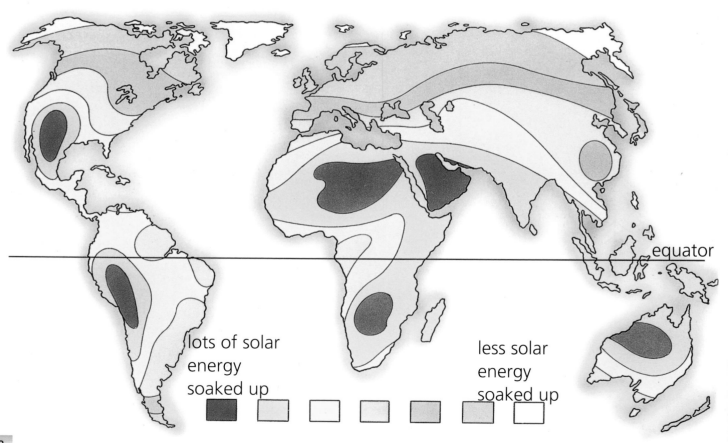

equator

lots of solar energy soaked up

less solar energy soaked up

FACT FILE

Light travels faster than anything else. It travels at a speed of 186,420 miles (300,000 km) a second. This means we usually see things as soon as they happen. But light takes thousands of years to reach us from far away in the universe.

◄ *A rainbow happens when sunlight shines through rain. The raindrops split the light into seven colors: red, orange, yellow, green, blue, indigo, and violet.*

FACT FILE

TOO MUCH SOLAR ENERGY

When the weather has been dry, trees dry out. Then they can catch fire in strong sunlight. In recent years, this has caused big forest fires in California, Spain, and France.

STORED SOLAR ENERGY

Wood is stored solar energy. Burning wood releases this stored energy as heat. Coal is formed from trees that died millions of years ago.

◀ *These are trees in a rain forest in Australia. The green chlorophyll in their leaves captures the energy of the sun, and uses it to make food for plants.*

Plants and Photosynthesis

All the plants and animals on the Earth rely on the sun. There is green chlorophyll in the leaves of plants. This chlorophyll captures the sun's energy. Plants use it to make food from water and carbon dioxide in the air. This process is called photosynthesis.

Solar Wind

About half the sun's energy turns into light. The rest of the energy is mostly infrared heat. There are also small electrically charged particles that come from the sun all the time. This is called solar wind. Storms around the sun can make these particles blow out suddenly.

The Solar Wind Particles

These particles shower the Earth. They can cause beautiful rainbow light in the sky near the North and South Poles. This colored light is called an aurora.

Bad Effects

However, the storms of solar wind particles can affect the Earth's magnetic field. This can cause problems to power cables, radio aerials, telephone lines, and satellites.

The Sun as a God

Many people in ancient times believed that the sun was a god. For instance, the Ancient Egyptians believed that the sun was a god who sailed across the sky in a heavenly ship.

FACT FILE

THE ICARUS STORY

In this Ancient Greek story, a young man named Icarus escaped from the island of Crete by flying. He used feathered wings held together by wax. But he flew too close to the sun. The heat melted the wax. The wings fell apart and Icarus fell to his death.

In this photograph, corn is drying in the sun. People have always used the sun to dry things, such as animals' skins, fish, leaves, and coffee beans. ▼

Eclipses

People in ancient times knew how important the sun was in their lives. Solar eclipses are when the sun disappears (partly or completely) behind the moon. This was terrifying. Ancient peoples worried that the sun might not come back.

Human Sacrifices

Some people in ancient times killed animals or humans to please the sun god. These were called sacrifices.

▲ *This little metal cart shows the sun being pulled by a horse. It comes from Denmark and is at least 3,000 years old. It tells us that the people who lived in Denmark long ago probably worshiped the sun as a god.*

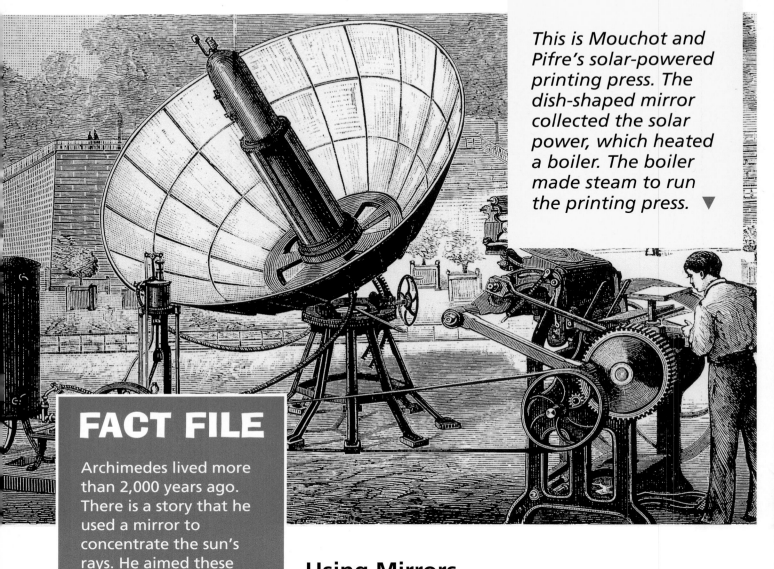

This is Mouchot and Pifre's solar-powered printing press. The dish-shaped mirror collected the solar power, which heated a boiler. The boiler made steam to run the printing press. ▼

Using Mirrors

In 1882, Augustin Mouchot and Abel Pifre invented a solar-powered printing press. A mirror dish concentrated the sun's rays onto a boiler. This made steam. The steam operated an engine to power the printing press. It could print 500 copies of a newspaper every hour.

Uses of Solar Power in History

- In 1774, Joseph Priestley concentrated the sun's rays to heat mercury oxide. It separated into mercury and oxygen. Oxygen was a newly discovered element.

- In the same century, Antoine Lavoisier built a solar-powered furnace. It was hot enough to melt metal.

- In 1891, Clarence M. Kemp invented a solar water heater. There are still half a million used today in California.

rays of light from the sun

lens

hole — burning in paper

▲ *A lens can concentrate or focus the sun's rays to burn a hole in paper.*

▲ *On a sunny day, four square yards of ground soak up one kilowatt of solar power. This is enough to run an electric toaster.*

This is a solar telescope, which can use the sun's energy to make measurements. ▼

SOLAR TECHNOLOGY

Simple Solar Collectors

There are several kinds of cheap, simple solar collectors.

- A cold frame is like a small greenhouse. The sun's rays pass through the glass to heat the air inside so that plants grow quickly.

- A solar dryer can dry vegetables (see the diagram below).

- A sheet of plastic can collect drinking water in the desert (see the opposite page).

A SOLAR DRYER
The sun shines on the glass panel. Cool air flows under it and is warmed up. The warm air then flows through the box and dries the vegetables. ▶

glass cover over blackened sheet

sunlight

cool air enters

pebbles hold down plastic sheet

dew evaporates

water collected in jar

TO COLLECT WATER IN THE DESERT

- *Dig a pit and place a jar in the bottom.*
- *Stretch a sheet of plastic over the pit early in the morning.*
- *The moisture condenses on the underside of the sheet and drips into the jar.*

◄ *Salt water is collected in pools. These pools are called saltpans. The sun warms the pans. The water evaporates. Salt crystals are left behind.*

A Typical Flat-Plate Collector

A flat-plate collector is a box covered with glass. The inside of the box is painted black. Water flows through a pipe that snakes through the box. The pipe is also painted black. This is because black absorbs heat well.

How Flat-Plate Collectors Work

Well-made flat-plate collectors can heat water to nearly boiling point. They are used to heat water for washing and heating. This is how they work:

- The sunlight heats the box.
- The hot air in the box heats the water in the pipes.

In northern countries, flat-plate collectors are on south-facing walls. This is so that they will collect the most light. This flat-plate collector is used to heat water at a hospital in the UK. ▼

This is a cutaway diagram of a flat-plate collector. As the water pipe snakes through the hot box, the water is heated.

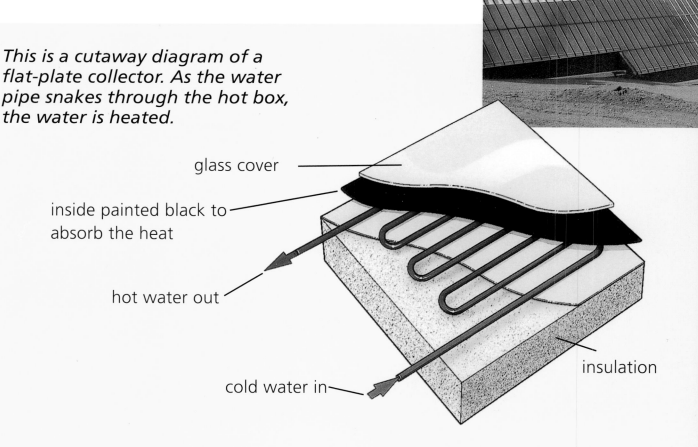

glass cover

inside painted black to absorb the heat

hot water out

cold water in

insulation

This photograph shows two types of flat-plate collector at a research center. The scientist is checking how well they work. He wants to find out which one is best. ▼

Concentrating Collectors

Concentrating collectors collect the sun's rays over a large area (see the photograph on page 21). Then the sunlight is focused into a small area. This makes very high temperatures (several thousand degrees).

Solar Furnaces and Heliostats

The type of concentrating collector shown in the photograph on page 21 is a solar furnace. Some of its mirrors move automatically to follow the sun. These types of mirror are called heliostats.

Trough Collectors

Trough collectors are more simple. Their mirrors do not move. This means they are less expensive to make, but they do not produce such high temperatures.

(see the photograph on page 21)

the photograph on page 21

FACT FILE

On the hill facing the huge, dish-shaped wall of mirrors are 63 heliostats. Each heliostat is 24 feet (7.3 m) high. These heliostats automatically follow the sun. They reflect the sun's rays on to the dish of mirrors. The dish of mirrors reflects back onto a target only 7 sq. in. (45 sq. cm). The sunlight is so concentrated that temperatures can go up to 6,872° F (3,800° C).

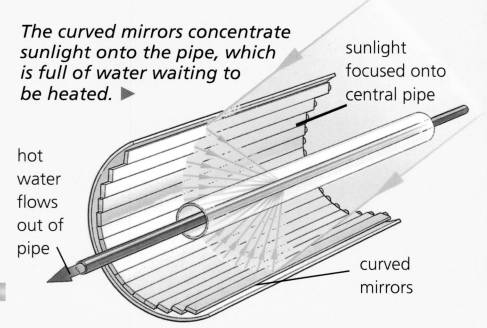

The curved mirrors concentrate sunlight onto the pipe, which is full of water waiting to be heated. ▶

hot water flows out of pipe

sunlight focused onto central pipe

curved mirrors

▲ Europe's largest solar furnace is in Odeillo, France. This photograph shows the huge dish of mirrors (called a parabola). The 63 giant heliostats are out of the picture, facing the parabola.

Solar Energy Generating Systems

The Solar Energy Generating Systems (SEGS) is made up of seven solar power plants in the Mojave Desert in California. Together, the SEGS sites make up the largest solar power plant in the world.

The SEGS plants cover more than 1,500 acres (607 hectares). They use a total of 90,000 mirrors to capture and collect sunlight to make into electricity. During the daytime, SEGS can generate 310 megawatts of electricity—enough to power 230,000 homes.

How SEGS Works

SEGS uses solar mirrors that capture the sun's energy to heat oil. The oil heats water to create steam, and the steam is sent into another building to turn a turbine. This powers a generator to make electricity. Finally, the electricity is sent by power cables to homes.

▲ *Solar mirrors are laid out in rows at SEGS to capture the sunlight.*

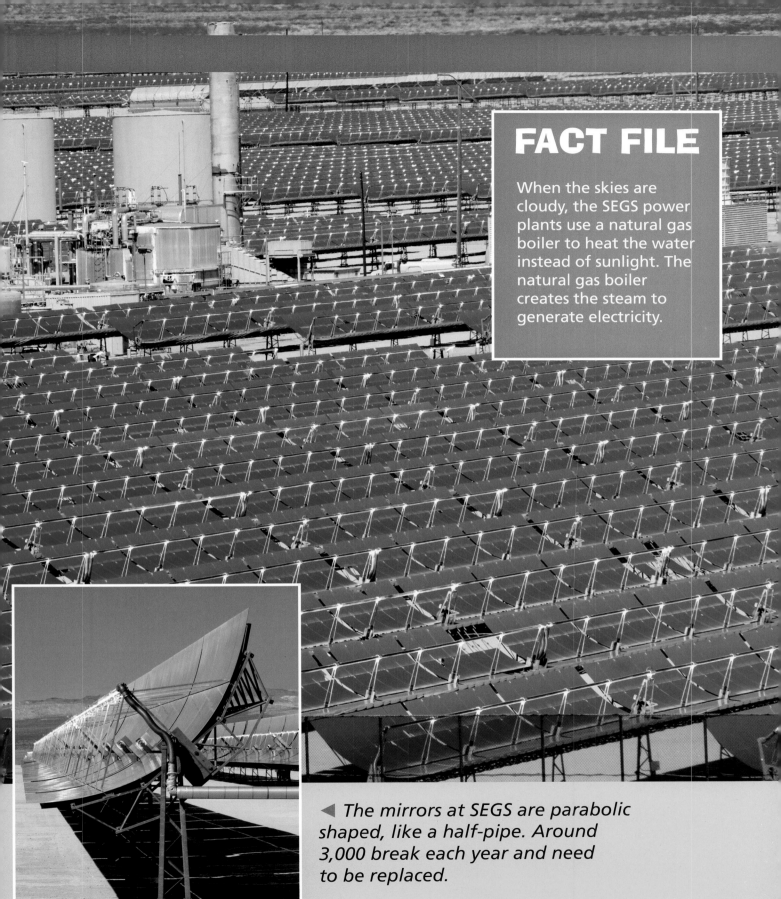

FACT FILE

When the skies are cloudy, the SEGS power plants use a natural gas boiler to heat the water instead of sunlight. The natural gas boiler creates the steam to generate electricity.

◀ *The mirrors at SEGS are parabolic shaped, like a half-pipe. Around 3,000 break each year and need to be replaced.*

23

◄ *A LIGHTHOUSE*
During the day, the solar panels soak up sunlight and make electricity. The electricity is stored in batteries until the lighthouse needs it after dark.

A Photovoltaic Cell or PV Cell

A photovoltaic cell is also called a solar cell. Just one cell the size of a fingernail makes a tiny electric current (see the diagram on the right).

What Solar Cells Can Power

- Three or four can power a pocket calculator.

- Several thousand can power a satellite in space.

Good and Bad Things About Solar Cells

There is no pollution from solar cells, and sunlight is free. However, the solar cells are expensive and do not produce a lot of power.

Solar cells are usually made from silicon. The energy from sunlight moves electrons through the cell. This makes an electric current. ▼

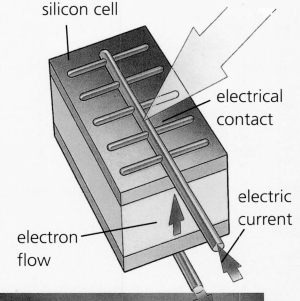

silicon cell

electrical contact

electric current

electron flow

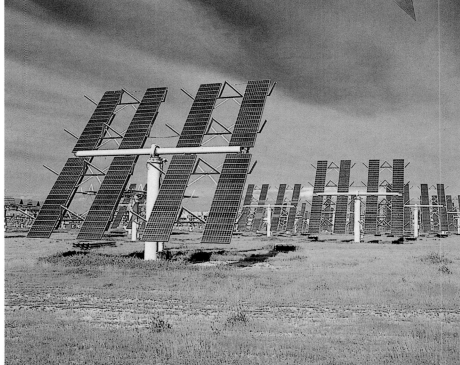

Solar panels make electricity at a solar power plant in California. ▶

Greenhouses

Greenhouses are made of glass. The sun's rays go through the glass and heat the air inside. The air is then trapped. Gardeners use greenhouses to grow plants that need plenty of warmth.

Other Buildings

Houses, offices, and other buildings can have large windows, too. Glass is cheap and it lets in sunlight to help warm the buildings.

Office buildings are often built with glass walls, like this one in Texas. ▼

FACT FILE

One of the world's most energy-efficient houses is in Nottinghamshire, UK. These are some of the things that are done:

- Rainwater is collected and stored.
- Waste water from bath and sinks waters the garden.
- Kitchen waste is turned into compost for the garden.
- The house is insulated to keep heat in.
- Electricity is made from solar panels.

An Energy-Efficient House

Glass lets in the sun's rays. On a hot day, it can be too hot. On a cold day, it can be too cold. The house in the diagram shows how sunlight falls on the big windows. It warms the air inside the house. The warm air rises, and cooler air from the top of the house flows down to the floor. This cool air cools the house. Building lots of energy-saving houses could save millions of tons of fossil fuels. Also, carbon dioxide is released when fossil fuels are burned. If too much carbon dioxide is released, the Earth's atmosphere may heat up too much. This is called global warming.

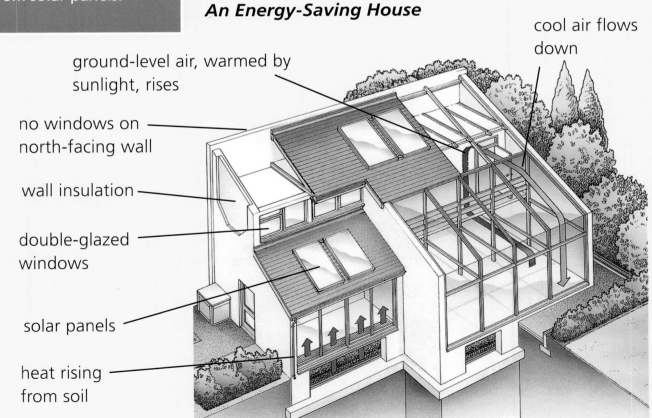

An Energy-Saving House

cool air flows down

ground-level air, warmed by sunlight, rises

no windows on north-facing wall

wall insulation

double-glazed windows

solar panels

heat rising from soil

A solar home is a house that uses solar energy efficiently for heating and lighting. Solar energy systems can be installed in new houses, but old houses can use solar energy, too.

An Old House in Denmark

The Bille family lived in an old house. It was heated using an oil-burning furnace. Then they installed four solar panels in the roof. These heated all the water in the summer and helped to heat some of the water in the winter. The family burned 132 gallons (500 L) less oil in a year than they did before.

The solar panels have to be kept clean to get the most energy from the sun. But only thick snow or very thick clouds stop them working completely. ▼

The white water tank sits next to the old green coal-burning furnace and farther to the right is the oil-burning furnace. ▶

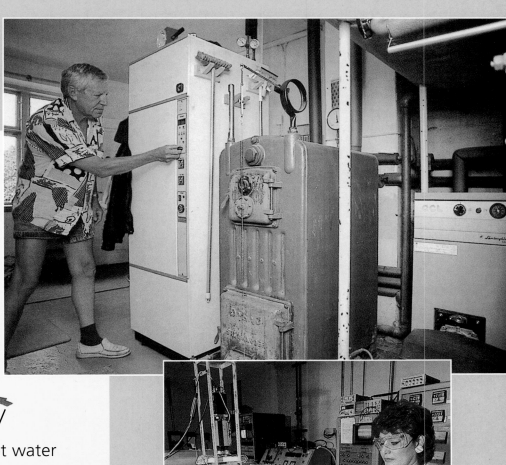

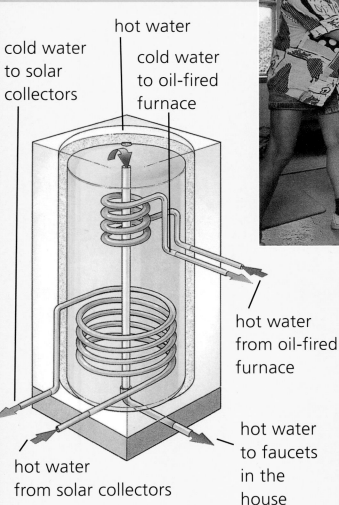

cold water to solar collectors

hot water

cold water to oil-fired furnace

hot water from oil-fired furnace

hot water from solar collectors

hot water to faucets in the house

▲ *There are two systems that heat the water in the water tank:*

● *The large coil (heated by solar collectors).*

● *The small coil (heated by an oil-burning furnace). This cuts in when there is not enough sunlight.*

▲ *Some solar houses use flat-plate collectors and photovoltaic cells. In this photograph, panels of photovoltaic cells are being made. Silicon for the cells is made from sand and rock.*

◀ *These street lights in Spain are powered by batteries that are charged with electricity from solar panels.*

▲ *Calculators, flashlights, and fans can be solar powered.*

FACT FILE

Bioluminescence is a cold light made by animals such as some beetles, flies, worms, deep-sea fish, and also some fungi.

They use it to:
- attract a mate
- attract some prey
- scare off attackers.

Batteries and Solar Power

Batteries are the most common portable power supply. But they run down. Solar panels are also portable and last a lot longer.

Portable Solar Power

Solar power is useful to run radios, telephones, and medical equipment in remote areas, where there is no electricity supply. So it is excellent for people such as explorers, scientists, and doctors.

Solar-Powered Lighting

Many types of lighting equipment use a mixture of solar power and batteries. Solar panels use solar energy to make electricity. The electricity is stored in batteries. It can then be used when it is dark. This kind of lighting is used all over the world.

In this picture, solar panels in the roof are powering the pump and filter to run the swimming pool. ▼

Air Pollution

There is lots of air pollution in some cities. Most of this pollution comes from car and truck engines.

Electric cars run on batteries, and do not produce air pollution. However, there are disadvantages to batteries. They are heavy, and they have to be charged with electricity every few miles. They also take hours to be fully charged.

Solar-powered cars would be cleaner and lighter, and they would not have these problems.

FACT FILE

Japan built its first solar-powered car in the 1990s. It had 640 solar cells powering an electric motor.

The first solar-powered aircraft flew in 1980. It was called the Solar Challenger and 16,128 solar cells powered its electric motors.

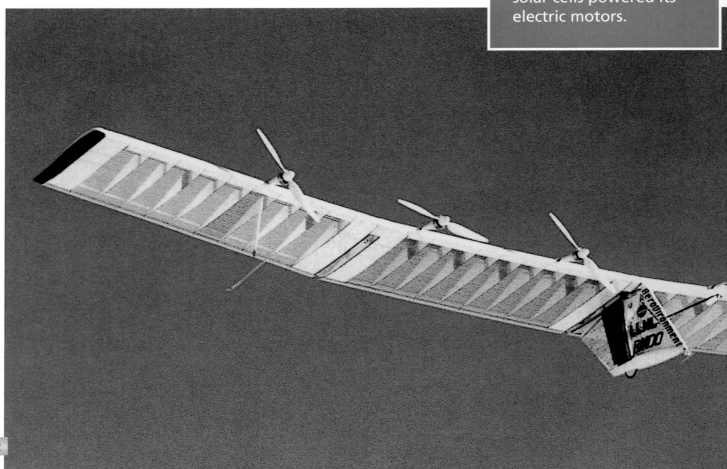

Advantages of Solar Power

Photovoltaic cells would be excellent to power a car.

- They have no moving parts to wear out.
- They use no fossil fuels.
- They do not need maintenance.

However, photovoltaic cells are not efficient enough to power a family car. They are also very expensive.

Pathfinder is a solar-powered aircraft. It has flown to a height of more than 65,600 feet (20,000 m) ▼

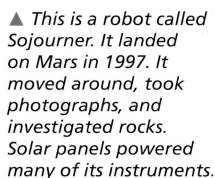

solar panel

camera

base station

ramp

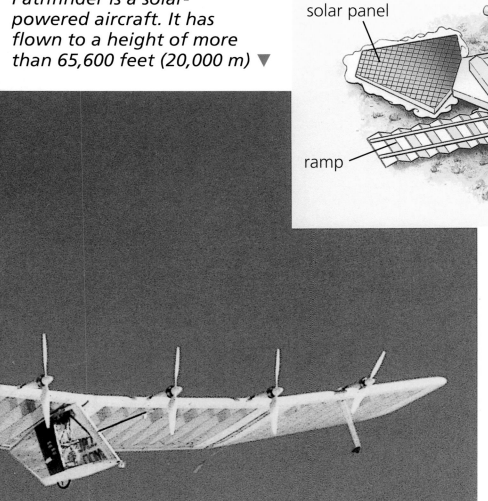

▲ *This is a robot called Sojourner. It landed on Mars in 1997. It moved around, took photographs, and investigated rocks. Solar panels powered many of its instruments.*

World Solar Challenge Car Race

Every two years, teams from all over the world meet in Australia to race their solar-powered cars. The race is 1,870 miles (3,010 km) long. The speed of the cars averages 42–56 mph (67–90 km/h). The purpose of the race is to encourage people to make solar-powered cars.

The Tokai Challenger won the World Solar Challenge in 2009. The dark blue top is made up of solar panels that power its electric motor. ▼

This car was made by Honda. It only weighed 276 pounds (125 kg). The solar panels are on the tail. ▼

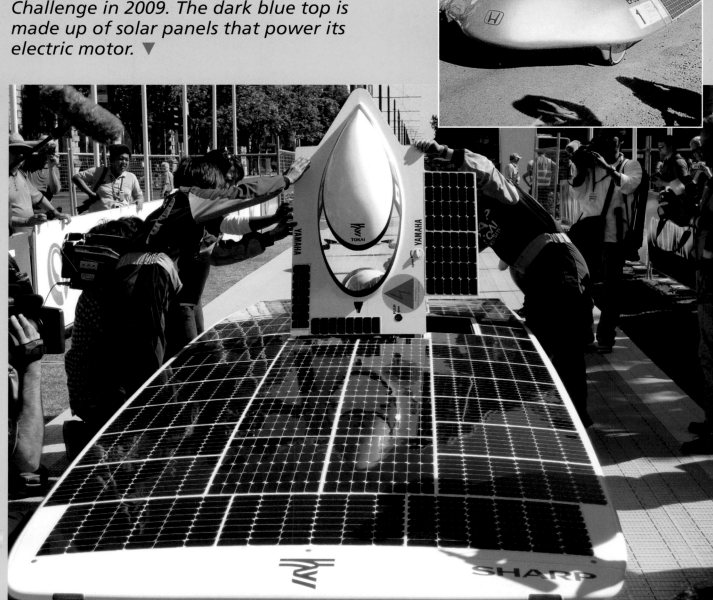

FACT FILE

The North American Solar Challenge (formerly called Sunrayce) is a solar car race for university teams in the United States and Canada. In 2008, the race took place along a route from Dallas, Texas, to Calgary, Alberta.

▲ *In 2008, a car called the Contiuum won the North American Solar Challenge. The total time it took was 51 hours, 41 minutes, and 53 seconds.*

Size, Shape, and Silence

Solar cars are small so that they are as light as possible. They are smooth so that they slip through the air. They are also silent.

A Japanese Winner

In 2009, Japan won the World Solar Challenge race in Australia using a car called the Tokai Challenger. The car was built by the Tokai University Solar Car team in Japan. It is covered with 65 square feet (6 sq. m) of solar panels and can reach up to 93 miles (150 km) per hour. However, it can hold only one passenger.

The Ups and Downs of Solar Power

The amount of solar energy that can be collected goes up and down, as clouds come and go. At night, there is no solar energy, so we need to be able to collect solar energy when the sun is out. Then we need to store it so we can use it later.

Storing Solar Energy

Solar energy can be stored in batteries. When the sun goes in, the batteries can power lights, pumps, and heating. When the sun comes out again, the solar energy from the solar panels can charge the batteries.

▲ The solar panels in the background are producing electricity to charge batteries.

▲ During the day, the sun warms the Earth. This solar energy controls our weather systems.

Solar Ponds

Solar heat can be stored in special ponds. The sides of the pond are thick. This is to stop heat from escaping. A typical solar pond is full of salty water. Salty water absorbs heat well.

During the day, sunlight warms the water. The saltiest water sinks to the bottom and holds the heat there. On cloudy days or at night, the hot water in the pond can be pumped out. It is pumped to a boiler where it is used to make steam. This steam is used to drive a turbine. The turbine powers a generator that makes electricity.

FACT FILE

NATURE'S SOLAR ENERGY STORES

Plants trap energy from sunlight in their leaves. If you burn leaves, they will give off heat.

Trees can store solar energy for years. If you burn wood, it gives off heat.

Coal, oil, and gas store solar energy for millions of years. If you burn them, they give off heat.

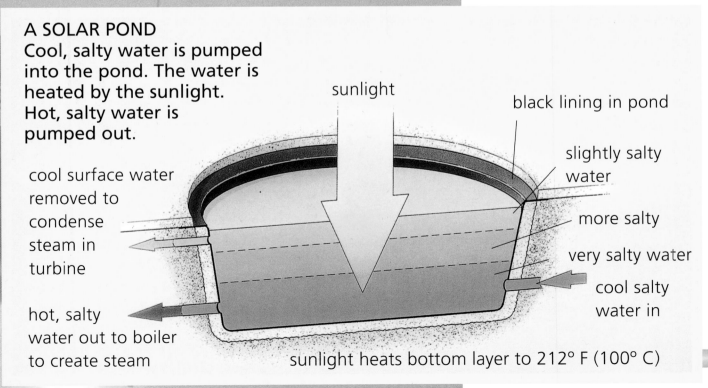

A SOLAR POND
Cool, salty water is pumped into the pond. The water is heated by the sunlight. Hot, salty water is pumped out.

sunlight

black lining in pond

slightly salty water

cool surface water removed to condense steam in turbine

more salty

very salty water

cool salty water in

hot, salty water out to boiler to create steam

sunlight heats bottom layer to 212° F (100° C)

A Radio Station in Mali

Mali is a country in Africa. Parts of Mali are a long way from any big towns. There are no telephones, newspapers, or mail services. How do people get information? One answer is the radio. But radio stations have to have a reliable electricity supply.

Radio Daande Douentza (RDD) is a solar powered radio station. It started in 1993. For most people, it is the only way they get information about health, farming, and news. It is partly supported by the charity Oxfam.

FACT FILE

Solar-powered cell phones can be used in countries where people live far away from a town and have no electricity supply to charge batteries. In 2009, solar cell phones were launched in Kenya. They are very popular.

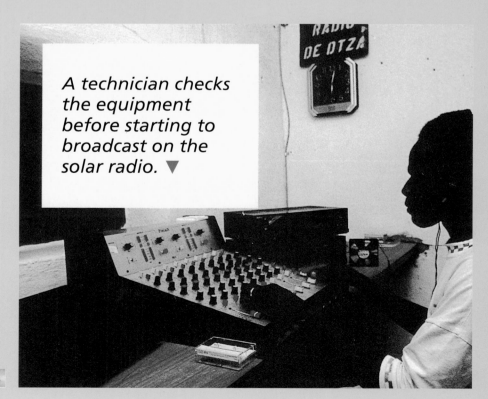

A technician checks the equipment before starting to broadcast on the solar radio. ▼

Radio Daande Douentza has solar panels in the roof to make its electricity. ▼

A radio presenter starts her broadcast. ▼

Success for Radio Daande Douentza

More than 85 percent of the local people listen to the radio station. In the first six months that it was running, the number of radios in this part of Mali doubled.

The radio station broadcast information about vaccinating children against disease. The number of children being vaccinated jumped from 30 percent to 50 percent of all children in the area.

NEW DEVELOPMENTS

Everyday Solar Power

As solar technology gets cheaper, more countries will be using the sun's energy to power their homes, stores, offices, and schools. Better ways of storing and transporting solar power will mean that it can be used even in places that do not get much sunlight.

Some big businesses, such as Walmart, are installing solar panels in the roofs of their stores in sunny places. Solar tiles that look like ordinary roof tiles have been developed for houses.

From 1991 to 1993, eight people lived inside this glass building, in Oracle, Arizona. It was called Biosphere 2. Heat and light were made by solar energy. The people stayed inside for two years, to test the conditions for a long time. ▼

FACT FILE

Biosphere 2 was the world's biggest closed-in living system. There were 3,800 different kinds of plants and animals inside. It was called Biosphere 2 because Biosphere 1 is Earth itself.

Artificial Trees

Scientists are trying to make an artificial tree that copies how leaves on a real tree gather energy using photosynthesis (see page 11). They want to make solar leaves that work together to turn sunlight into power. They also want to convert wind energy from the rustling of leaves into electricity.

A man named Ross Lovegrove invented the Solar Tree. The leaves on the tree have built-in solar panels that generate electricity from sunlight. A row of Solar Trees was installed on a street in Vienna, Austria, and may be used in other cities.

▲ *The Solar Tree has solar panels that collect sunlight in the daytime, then light up the streets when it gets dark.*

This diagram shows how sunlight heats the air in plastic tunnels. The hot air rises up a chimney. As it rises, it turns a turbine that is connected to a generator that makes electricity. ▼

Desert Power

Solar power may be used more and more in hot desert areas to capture the energy of the sun. Panels of solar cells can be laid out across the sand. These can provide a great deal of electricity. Where deserts are near the sea, electricity could be used to turn sea water into drinking water.

There are plans to build a huge network of solar power plants in the Sahara desert, in North Africa. The network will cover an area almost as big as New Jersey. It could produce enough electricity to power all of Europe. But engineers must find a way to build cables that can send the electricity hundreds of miles away to countries that need it.

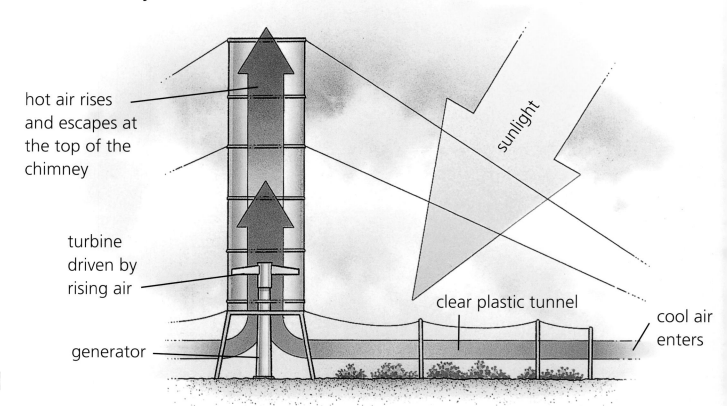

hot air rises and escapes at the top of the chimney

sunlight

turbine driven by rising air

clear plastic tunnel

cool air enters

generator

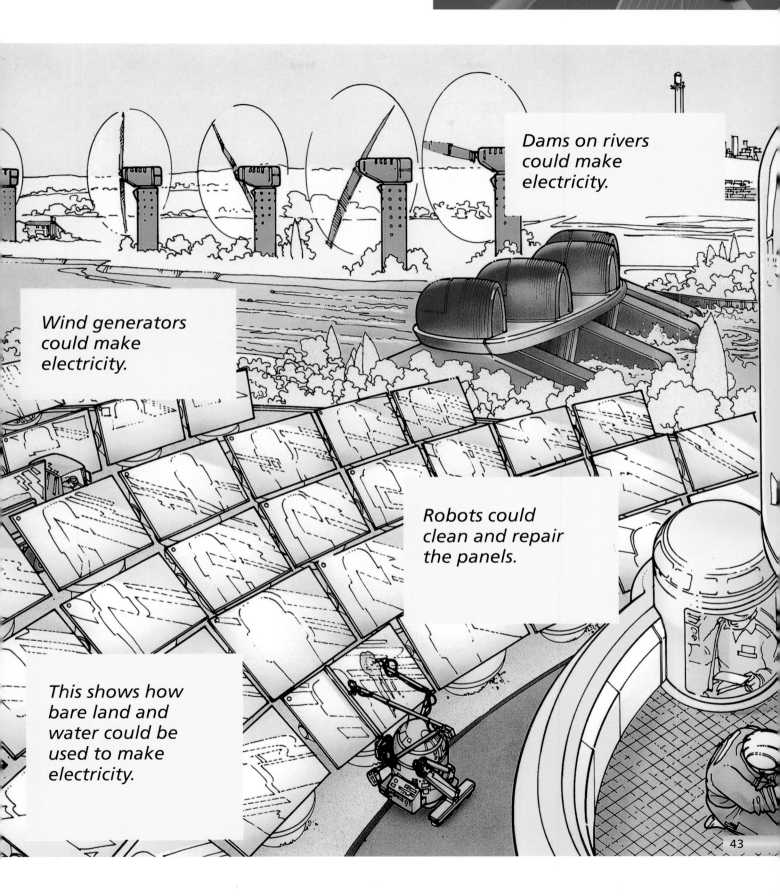

Dams on rivers could make electricity.

Wind generators could make electricity.

Robots could clean and repair the panels.

This shows how bare land and water could be used to make electricity.

◀ *A small power station in space.*

◀ *The International Space Station uses an acre of solar panels. These provide electricity for its computers and instruments.*

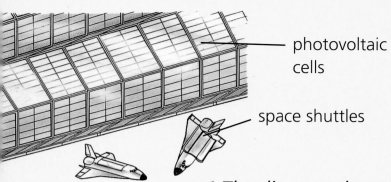

photovoltaic cells

space shuttles

◄ *The diagram shows a giant power plant of photovoltaic cells in space. The cells would be kept pointing at the sun by automatic instruments. The power would be beamed down to Earth. Another idea is to have a number of small power plants like the one shown on page 44.*

FACT FILE

SUN SAILS

A Russian teacher drew some designs for sun sails nearly a hundred years ago. He designed a spacecraft that was a lot like the ones used on the moon—about 60 years after he had thought of the idea.

A Solar Collector in Space

The atmosphere around the Earth is full of dirt, which blocks some solar energy. There is dust from volcanoes and sandstorms.There is pollution from cars, factories, and power stations.

A solar collector or photovoltaic panel would get much more solar energy if it was outside the Earth's atmosphere. This would mean building a power plant in space. It would use solar panels to make electricity. This would be changed into microwaves and sent to Earth. It would then be changed back into electricity.

Solar Sails

Future spaceships might use huge sails, to be blown along by the pressure of the sun and solar winds. Many space agencies such as NASA are testing solar sails made from light materials such as aluminum.

GLOSSARY

Atmosphere The gases that surround a planet, moon, or star.

Atom A very small particle. (A particle is a tiny part of something.)

Aurora The rainbow lights in the sky near the North and South Poles.

Carbon dioxide A gas in the air made from plants and animals breathing, and from burning fossil fuels.

Concentrating collector A large mirror or lens that gathers sunlight and focuses it in one spot.

Electromagnetic waves Waves that have both electric and magnetic parts.

Electron A particle with an electric charge.

Element A very simple substance.

Energy Able to do work.

Evaporate To turn from a liquid to a gas.

Flat-plate collector A flat panel that changes sunlight into heat.

Focus The point where light rays come together.

Fossil fuels Fuels formed millions of years ago from the remains of plants and animals.

Helium An element formed inside very hot stars.

Hydrogen The lightest element in the universe.

Infrared Electromagnetic waves that transfer heat.

Kilowatt A unit of electrical power (1,000 watts).

Magnetic field The area around a magnet where the magnet affects things.

Microwaves Radio waves used for sending signals and for cooking.

Nuclear fission When a heavy nucleus splits apart. This releases a lot of energy.

Nuclear fusion When nuclei hit each other so fast that they join together. This releases a lot of energy.

Nucleus The particle or particles at the center of an atom.

Photosynthesis A green plant's process of making food using the energy of the sun.

Photovoltaic cell A device that converts sunlight into electricity.

Recycling Using things again instead of throwing them away.

Silicon An element that is used to make solar cells.

Solar cell Another name for a photovoltaic cell.

Solar collector Anything that receives energy from the sun and converts it into another form of energy.

Solar energy Energy from the sun.

Solar furnace A type of concentrating collector.

Solar power plant A power plant that makes electricity from the sun's energy.

Solar wind Particles that stream out from the sun.

Watt A unit of power.

FURTHER INFORMATION

Further Reading

The Kids' Solar Energy Book Even Grown-ups Can Understand
by Tilly Spetgang and Malcolm Wells
Imagine Publishing, 2009

Powering the Future: New Energy Technologies
by Eva Thaddeus
University of New Mexico Press, 2010

Solar Energy: Running on Sunshine
by Amy S. Hansen
PowerKids Press, 2010

Web Sites

http://home.clara.net/darvill/altenerg/solar.htm

http://science.howstuffworks.com/solar-cell.htm

http://www.eere.energy.gov/topics/solar.html

Power plant produces several million watts.

Family house uses a few thousand watts.

Washing machine: 2,500 watts

Electric iron: 1,000 watts

Lightbulb: 100 watts

ENERGY CONSUMPTION
The use of energy is measured in joules per second, or watts. Different machines use up different amounts of energy. The diagram on the right gives a few examples. ▶

GLOSSARY